Words & Paper

Mukisa N. A. Kibaya

ISBN 978-1-300-53449-5

To God be the Glory, for allowing me to lay down my burdens
To living, loving and learning

Poem List

1. Headache
2. Quiet Toast
3. Gumbo
4. Gray Area
5. At The End
6. Where Are You?
7. Careless, Not Helpless
8. Higher Learning Letter
9. Shawna
10. Thinking Freestyle
11. Writing Through The Pain
12. Travel
13. If Wishes Came True
14. YOLO
15. Hijabi
16. Coffee Is
17. Exodus 3:14
18. Tears
19. Profoundly Unfounded Confusion
20. Getting It Together
21. I Cannot Just
22. Facebook Confession #2

1 Headache

Pain
O sweet bless-ed
Oh so press-ed
Pain.
It's Gwen Stefani wanting to make
The Sweet Escape
And rape
My normalcy.
Omarion's Obsession
My head-head-a-boom- boom- tap.
Trapped!
In school's swirling vortex,
Waiting to be ejected into
My space by the bell.
Ibuprofen seems an unattainable goal.
It's to help me be better,
Or so I've been told.
So I've got this pounding
SCREAMING on the inside
Hopeless on the outside
But my side
On this divide
Is I have to ride
This out
My pride
Lies in that
I've tried
Ignoring
The boring
In my hood
Holes of dread,
With knowledge and memories
Niagara Falling out,
Leaving a pensive drought
With cacti of elementary school
And roadrunners of memories forgotten,
All
From
A
Pain
In

The Brain.

2 Quiet Toast

I was bread this morning
Popping out of the toaster at 6 am.
I headed to the bathroom
For my peanut butter and jelly,
And teeth that are clean.
I washed the crumbs off my
Crunchy face,
Just wondering.
When was my other coming?
Was he slumming
Chasing ho after ho
Like all the garden tools were running
Away?
Where are the men boys who mingle
And are really single
& need a good woman girl?
I don't need a guy
Who wonders why
I get hurt
When his theme song
Is "I'm A Flirt".
Ambition,
Honesty, and intelligence
Are what I desire
And require
In my other
Who is
No significant yet.
My peanut butter
And jelly are in place
Clean teeth, clean face.
Before I put on
My plastic wrap
To look so fresh and fly,
I write this and
Wonder why...
I wish so hard
With quiet,
Not-so-desperate
Desperation.

3 Gumbo

I have never tasted it
But I've seen it
With my four eyes
You start with a big pot of waking up
Slice and dice the morning routine
Which is not so routine
Shred and add your wardrobe
Add 1 cup of school
Mix with dancing and happy music
Scramble the confidence of feeling good
And looking mah-velous,
Drop in your best wedges.
Anticipate hunger!
You want to eat the
Day, the moment.
No seriously, eat something!
No hunger allowed!
Mix vigorously,
Put on the stove
On a low, laid-back flame.
Cover with a top,
So you don't partake early.
Now turn up to a hot,
Eager flame!
You're ready to eat
Finally, cool in the
Workout fridge.
Enjoy!

4 Gray Area

Push and pull
Tug of war
Between my future and my heart
I don't know if I can make it through
All I can do
Is try
While I cry
Tears
Of agony
Of boredom
Of small triumph
Of big trial
I've had enough
Of this emotional rollercoaster
Tears sometimes run over
You might need a coaster
Not to ruin your pristine table
That you call life
That I why I hesitate
To tell you my problems
There's no way that you or I can solve them
My anxieties trapped inside
I keep them imprisoned
I don't even know if they'll get parole
To play the role
Of a reminiscing joke
I'll remember someday of this
And laugh
Genuinely, with no laugh track
But until then, I'm stuck
In an ugly impasse
This is the fact
That has me tripping
Like untied shoelaces
Can't admit to faces
That I'm in the place
I'd never thought I'd be.

5 At The End

If you're reading this
Or hearing this
You know now
That I stand at the end
The end of complacence
I have tried my patience
Wondering when answers will come
Looking up most days at the sun
Its rays shining brilliant
Mocking my sadness
How long I prayed
Knowing if I stayed
Right here
In this same spot
Blessings will drop
In the form of answers.
But I know now
That things don't always come to you
When you sit and wait for them
Sometimes you have to go on a chase.
So just call me Dream Chaser.

6 Where Are You?

I have been looking for you everywhere!
Not just here,
But there.
I can't reach the high places yet
But I regret
To inform you that I've been looking
In low places too,
Not wanting to limit you
And your movements
You are heaven sent,
But sent to where?
I don't know!
But the places I will go
To find you
Are infinite in my mind.
I am limited by time space
And all the distracting faces
I find during my searching.
I am desperate to hurting
For a sign that tells me
My wait and search is worthwhile.
I won't be a folder in your file
Cabinet of conquests
For I am nothing less
Than a queen.
So I peep my scenes
Like an editor for a movie,
For I am closer to a director
And I'm farther from a groupie.
But all this is redundant,
You'd know that if you knew me.
But I don't know you,
Which is probably why it's so hard.
You're probably not walking
Down Douglas Boulevard
So our paths could randomly cross.
So I huff
And I puff.
I wish
And I wait,
Seeing all these couples,

Hoping for the day
That it will be soon for me.
For love is truly free,
I have so much to give
Hopefully I'll live
As a love supplier.
Good man, tell me where you are,
So I can ship my love.

7 Careless, Not Hopeless

I admit to many mistakes
Many failings
But you'd be searching forever
To find someone perfect
To judge my indiscretions
I can say I've learned my lessons
Time and time again
Just be patient, my friend.
One day you'll come to your test
And we'll find you not at your best
And you will know what I meant
In this moment.
So own it and be whoever you are
Because by far,
You'd be the only you
And I'd be the only me
So I feel free
To make mistakes
In my outstanding fashion
To repent for them
With my extraordinary passion
To get down on my knees
And pray for a better day
That God may grant me
After a period of disarray
Or He may say,
"Your test isn't over.
Come, be a little closer.
Lean not on your own strength,
For my strength surpasses all."
Now and forever,
I will stand tall
Knowing I have divine favor
My wrongdoing has been paid for
By the blood of the lamb.
Before the approach of my next mistake
Please, I ask you to take
A minute and pray
For me
And for you too,
To who or whatever you pray to,

So that you understand me
When you find yourself in my shoes.

8 Higher Learning Letter

Dear Powers That Be,
I want to learn.
I want to feel free
To engage myself
In this dynamic process
That is called learning
Instead of yearning
To stoop to
Hostile confrontation
Because my education
Has reduced me to
A cynical idiot
Knowing of what I **should** know
Without the knowledge
To attain such information.

Powers That Be,
I wonder if you know me.
I am more than nine numbers
Stuck on me when I entered
This here your university.
I am more than the classes,
That I took, passed and failed.
I am a person in need
Of guidance
Of patience
Of empathy.

You Powers should understand,
I was so close to throwing this all away.
It's your time to take my hand
And tell me that I should hang in there
That all these teary days
And all these sleepless nights
Are promissory notes
That I can cash in for my future.
That I can know that
This isn't the end
But only the middle
Of an arduous process

Nonetheless,
I will be emotionally supported.

Please act accordingly.
Sincerely, Mukisa

9 Shawna

~For/To Erin (Kinnerk) Sherrow

So many miles away from home
Thinking about what you've done
Good or bad, you're still my friend
There 16 years until the very end
My PiC-S
I pray that you make it
I pray that you succeed
Even though you'll always be
Hundreds of miles away from me
Don't mind my sighs
Or rolling eyes
Because I love you
That's all
And I want you to be okay
For you to find a way
To happiness
No matter where it takes you
And who you walk with
Because you have always been
On my path to happy
With pineapples
And random hand gestures
So I say to you
"Smile, baby!"
The best is yet to come
Have a little fun
Because we are young
And that's what young people do
But I know we are not up to trouble
Or are we?
Doesn't matter.
Either way,
I'll stay
Right here
Just waiting
With random trivia
And sambusas.
To solve crime
And have good times
With you.

10 Thinking Freestyle

Since the cheese stands alone
Call me cheddar
I do it like I do it
'Cuz nobody does it better
I'll be standing right here
No matter the type of weather
Because I'm a heavyweight
And you're lighter than a feather
I'm not just talking power
When I say my weight's heavy
I'm a big girl
And I tend to rock steady
Don't rush me!
I make moves when I'm ready.
You could find me in the kitchen
Cookin' meatballs and spaghetti
Or you could find me
Between the pages of a book
Perhaps writing rhymes
All these lines without a hook
The words that I form
Will leave all y'all shook
Excuse me, I mean shaken
I'm sorry I don't reflect
All the grammar that I've taken
All these lessons that I've learned
Have my brain straight achin'
But I have to be proud
Of the progress that I'm makin'
So I don't know why
Some are afraid to learn
Don't think to play with fire
And not get burned
Every risk that one takes has a consequence
Have an opinion about something
Get your ass off the fence
The world keeps turning
Whether one likes it or not
Life can be so much more
Than a home or a block
My life ain't about

The clothes I got
The shoes I rock
Or even the jewelry I cop
It's about learning the best things are free
Love, affection and trips to the library
Trying to be the best I can be
In spite of those who hate so magnificently
I'm not trying to be like her
The girl from around your way
I am my own woman
So hear me when I say
Mukisa Kibaya is who I am today
I am not her
God made us that way
I am a unique creation
Compare me to myself
Don't even bother!
Leave that ruler on the shelf
I don't wanna be measured
By how I conform
But by whether I can weather
Some terrible storms
Don't measure me by currency
I can't be bought
I'm just a woman with a pen
Thinking some thoughts.

11 Writing Through The Pain

Nothing says Happy Tuesday like a migraine
I write this in semi-darkness
Blinds over the windowpane
For the outside light
Is just too bright
So I cower from the daytime
And wait for the night
Creating quite a dark illusion of normalcy
Wishing I could live my live normally
Instead of wondering
When the next pain's gonna strike
Will it bring me to my knees
And bring tears to my eyes?
How do I explain this
To someone who hasn't felt such agony?
How do I explain something tragic
To one who hasn't experienced such tragedy?

12 Travel

Ever get out of a plane
And it's two hours later
Energy is kind of low
Like the basement button on an elevator
Feel like I ran really hard
From start to finish
I should be in a relationship
But my heart's not in it
I guess I'm too ambitious
I have goals to reach
Places to go
Promises to keep
Peeps are getting engaged
But I feel no pressure
Keep myself under lock and key
Like a hidden treasure
I also have standards
That I don't apologize for
Lies, blasphemes and manipulation
I don't have time for
Sanity and expression
That's what I rhyme for

13 If Wishes Came True

What if I wished
On a shooting star
And every wish I made
Came true near and far
What would I wish for?
What would you wish?
What would be your answer
If I asked you this?

No guessing for wishes
I've already made a list
Check out this wishy rhyme
Tell me if they're ludicrous
I wish that everyone
Had a place to stay
A place where they could hang their hat
A place for their head to lay
I wish that every and any one
Was gainfully employed
Every job would be legit
The trap wouldn't have our girls and boys
I wish that every boy and girl
Would have a loving home
So they'd have an idea of love
Instead of acting grown
I wish that every single child
No matter their neighborhood of residence
Could go to good schools and eat healthy foods
And rise to their levels of decadence
Where preparing for the future would take precedence
I wish, I wish
That everybody could live right
Not go looking for trouble
At odd hours of the night
Just the thought of such behavior
Would give them all a fright

14 YOLO

You Only Live Once
Drake said that's the motto
I believe that
So Jesus I do follow
People doing reckless stuff
But inside they are hollow
I wonder what would happen
If they were judged for all of
That stuff
That they do
Do they know
Jesus died for you
And you and you
Yes, you too
And all of the people
In your crew
He gave His life
And today He rose
Giving my life to Him
Isn't much, I suppose
He is the reason
I write this prose
Excuse me this is poetry
Please don't stop my flow
Because the Spirit flows
Flows in me
He is the Light
The Light I need
He paid for all my sins
I have been freed
So now I shall praise Him
Glorify Him indeed
I only live once
God gave me this life
He gave His son Jesus Christ
So I try to live right
You Only Live Once
Drake said that's the motto
I walk a thin line
Evil lurks in its grotto
Trying to master me

But I say heck no
With Jesus on my side
Sin can't play me like Nintendo

15 Hijabi

~To those who are judged

I write because
It's my way
I write because
I need some faith
From solace
Nestled
Nicely in hands
Sparked by neurons
I write because
I am
I write because
You are
We walk different
Paths of faith
That are never straight
Because we cry out
Different names
When we look to sky
Modesty calls us both
Sounding differently though
Your hair
Rarely sees the sun
While I am the one
With hair blowing
In the breeze
I fall to my knees
In wooden pews
While you
Pray on mats
Facing the rising sun
I am not of you
So I cannot
Judge your truth
God calls me
To love you
To need you
To respect you
So I write
To right wrongs
To right judgments

To right
Every insult
Every look
Every stare
Every change of facial expression
Because when I
Take my scarf
And walk into
A crowd
I am you
I write because
I was wrong
I write because
I want to better
I write because
We need to get it together
I write I write I write

16 Coffee Is

Coffee is
Beans
Fair trade
Unfair monies
Cash crop picked from the Motherland's soil
Brown skinned folks around the globe
Stoop so low
For pennies
And Starbucks
Wishes go to stars
For more bucks
Hunger tucked in the stomachs
Of coffee pickers
As greed over greed over greed
Strips them of their share
I hardly argue
That trade is ever fair
Since someone always pays the price.

Coffee is
Skin
That comes in all shades and flavors
Thanks to cream and sugar and syrup
Flavors from everywhere
Combining in one cup
From strong and black
To Boston Crème
Hot coffee toddy
Each cup
Tasty to someone
Of value to someone
So discount them not
They are all full price

Coffee is
WOW
Caffeine shooting through vessels
Soothing the vessel
Of my thoughts
Allowing me to
Smile

Feel happy
Not care
Keep my feathers unruffled
Focusing on what is to be done
Instead of what is done
To me
Free of reactivity
To pursue any activity
I wish
Knowing this
That coffee is

17 Exodus 3:14

You said to Moses
You are who You are
I am just a passenger
You're the driver of the car
Without You
I couldn't go far
Because You have the keys

You are who You are
There's no way to deny
That
Not speak or think of Your love
I couldn't try
That
They say
Prayers go up
Blessings come down
Your cross is my love
Your love is my crown
You are who You are
Lover
Fighter
Shelter
Provider
Father
Son
Holy Spirit
One
God said to Moses, "I am who I am."

18 Tears

Tears drip down
From sad eyes
Which confirmed things
That my brain didn't want to believe
I stay hoping
Hoping for a change
Hoping for light
For light to shine on me
For light to stay a while
To see the sun
I hoped for
Open blinds
To claim what little light
That is outside the picture window
I hoped for bright green walls
Shining from fluorescent light bulbs
Something to show
Something to show occupancy
Something to show care
Something to show life

19 *Profoundly Unfounded Confusion*

*I think God aligns us far greater
Than we can EVER understand
It's all a part of His master plan
Everything happens in His time
But why does it feel like a crime
To wait and see
What he has for me
Because I have no answers
As time keeps marching on
And I keep dancing
To the same darn song
Though I am not
A character on Psych
But everything in gray
I cannot settle down
Into another day
Call it a flaw
A vice
Whatever you will
The fact remains
I can't sit still
Without knowing
Growing
Without a destination
Following His light
For He planted me in the ground
So what am I to do now?*

20 Getting It Together

I wish I could hate you
Hating you would be the easiest thing right now
I'd get angry
I'd get silent
I wouldn't talk to you
I would delete your number
I would unfriend you on Facebook
Erase any existence of you in my life
And become an expert at it
So much so
That I would run into you
Two years later
Not even remembering you
Not even remember why I hated you in the first place
Instead I'm just emotional
Emotional as in
I am just feeling too many fucking things right now
So please don't ask me if I'm ok
Angry that we have come to this
That I have come to this
Gotten into a situation so weird
That I was hesitant to tell anybody
Just knowing in my gut that they couldn't advise
Angry that I didn't stop things sooner
That I willingly drove over a cliff
Knowing that there was a possibility the road would end
But driving on hope anyway
Sad that your plethora of sorries
Makes me feel more like a hooker
Than a pimp named Sweetback and a ho stroll ever could
Well damn it I'm not sorry
I'm not sorry
That for one moment
I had everything I wanted
With a man
After so many years
Of telling myself that it could never happen
I'm just hurt
That this one time
That this one time
That this one time

I wanted to truly fall apart
I had to pull it together
That we didn't think it through
Hurt that
I feel reduced
To an impulsive action
Instead of a premeditated plan
Hurt that
I can't answer your questions
Questions that I never even thought
To ask myself
But I have made up my mind
Not to be guilty
Not to feel guilty
For I see the guilt
On your face
On your shoulders
I refuse to be your accomplice
To a crime
That you are turning yourself in for
I am much better than that
Much better than regret
Much better than waiting to figure out
What it is that you want to do
Much better than
Looking to you for answers
Because unfortunately
My dear brother
You just screwed yourself
Mind, body and soul
And that's a toll
I have no change to pay
If I thought I could say this to you
To your face
And you understand what I mean
I would
But I know
That I have yet
To look a man
To date a man
Knowing that he's The One
He will propose

That I'm wifey
Church, reception, the end.
Married.
Where do you get that idea?
Where do you find that woman
That you know to settle down with?
Because people have a way to surprise.
I mean, look here.
I never thought this would happen.
That we would come to this.
I would just be happy
Meeting someone,
Committing to someone
That I know enough about
To spend the rest of my life
Getting to know him more.
But maybe that's the difference between us,
When it comes to these matters,
Matters of the heart.
I just want to know enough,
And you want to know it all.
I hope you find what you are looking for.
And I hope it is always what you want.
And I hope I can get around to hating you.
I would settle for not liking you at all.
Maybe it wouldn't bother me so much,
This wouldn't bother me so much,
If I could just walk away
For good.
Because things will never be the same.
We dropped and broke the mirror.
You're trying to glue it together,
All I see are the cracks.

21 I Cannot Just

~ for @JJ_Bola

I cannot just
Close my eyes
To the sight in front of me
I cannot just
Sail past the begging man
Asking for some spare change
I cannot just
Pretend that things are changing
Wars are still secret
Neighborhoods are changing
Changing like five ones
For a five dollar bill
Still
I notice
The white people from cross town
Are now the white people down the way
Will be the white people down the street
Eventually the white people down the block
While all the melanin leaves the neighborhood
Bit by bit
I cannot just-ify
The guilt I feel
When I hear my country
Being called to task
For murders of innocent lives
And for what I say
When does power
When does control
Mean more than a life
Mean more than lives
I cannot just
Forget what I know
Praying to God for a better day
For mercy on Judgment day
For those who care not
Who thought
Bloodshed in the darkness didn't count
I cannot just
Hide from where I am from
Because those who lead that beautiful place

Think only of themselves
YES I AM UGANDAN
Despite who leads it
Despite who mistreats it
My ancestors' bones will always rest there
I cannot just
Pick up a gun
And be an avenger
To defend the defenseless
As much as I want to
All I can do is pray
All I can do is write
All I can do is speak
For those souls
Who have no reason
To just die in vain
All I can do is say
FREE CONGO

22 *Facebook Confession #2*

~ for Donté Partee/Mic Dick Her

-Think back to homecoming, either Junior or Senior year, I'm not sure. But I asked you to dance and you was grinding on me and all that, and I thought to myself, "OMG, you're my friend, there is absolutely no reason I should be getting an erection.' Forgive me, I am male LOL. Because of your background, I find myself wondering if I could get you to twerk to a juke song that sample the Lion King's "Circle of Life," featuring myself, Future, and Waka Flocka. Don't act like that wouldn't be the shit. LOL. I know I told you I would take to the studio when I be recording and all that, but truthfully, I haven't been recording much recently. However, I'm back in all grind mode now, so I'll let you know when it's time to go. Just make sure you can hang because I do most of my recording at night.

DON'T STOP POP THAT DON'T STOP POP THAT POP THAT POP THAT
Boy I love the way you do me do me do me do me do me do me
DON'T STOP POP THAT DON'T STOP POP THAT POP THAT POP THAT
Boy I love the way you do me do me do me do me do me do me

Just call me a lyrical DJ
I write all the hits that he play
Because the turntables do what me say
C'mon na pon dat replay
Y'all know how to rep your hood
Lemme show you how to do it good
One up for my pipo from Chi City
We grind with grit
We smile real pretty
Two up for my UG fam
Do that Kiganda dance if you can

DON'T STOP POP THAT DON'T STOP POP THAT POP THAT POP THAT
Boy I love the way you do me do me do me do me do me do me
DON'T STOP POP THAT DON'T STOP POP THAT POP THAT POP THAT
Boy I love the way you do me do me do me do me do me do me

I call this hit Afrobeat ratchet
If you feel the fever
Gwan head and catch it

Wine your hips just a lickle bit
If you a lickle flexible
Gwan do a split
If you are hungry
Go get some emmere
Mama will feed you
Matooke and sauce
All night it will keep you

DON'T STOP POP THAT DON'T STOP POP THAT POP THAT POP THAT
Boy I love the way you do me do me do me do me do me do me
DON'T STOP POP THAT DON'T STOP POP THAT POP THAT POP THAT
Boy I love the way you do me do me do me do me do me do me

Na na na na na na na na naaa....kambere nawe
Na na na na na na na na naaaaa..... kambere nawe
Oh oh, Kambere nawe
Eh eh, Kambere nawe
Ohhhh oh, kambere nawe
Ehhhhhh eh, kambere nawe

I need a ryde or die chick
I like to rock Prada suits and my a **is fat
I need a ryde or die chick
I push a Cadillac truck with my friends in the back
I need a ryde or die chick
Smoke 'dro, drink liquor, like to uhhh! 'til I uh!
I need a ryde or die chick
I rock a icy ass chain with a earring in my tongue